# UNICORN

## COLOR BY NUMBER

BELONGS TO

- - - - - - - - - - - - - - - - - - - - - - - - - - - - - -

BY NIKKI SHARMA

# Are you ready to color the Pages!!

# Let's do it...

1=Green　　　　2=Brown　　　　3=Yellow　　　　4= Blue

5=Orange　　　　6=Purple　　　　7=Pink　　　　8=Red

1=Green        2=Yellow        3= Pink        4= Purple

5=Orange       6=Red           7=Blue         8=White

1=Green    2=Red    3=Yellow    4= Blue
5=Orange   6=Purple   7=Pink    8=White

1=White    2=Brown    3=Yellow    4= Blue

5=Orange    6=Red    7=Purple    8=Pink

1=Green        2=Brown        3=Yellow        4= Blue

5=Orange        6=Purple        7=Pink        8=White

1=Green 2=Red 3=Yellow 4= Blue

5=Orange 6=Purple 7=Pink 8=White

1=Green    2=White    3=Yellow    4= Blue

5=Orange    6=Purple    7=Pink

1=Orange     2=Brown     3=Yellow     4= Blue

5=White     6=Purple     7=Pink     8=Black

1=Green        2=Brown        3=Yellow        4= Blue

5=Orange        6=Purple        7=Pink        8=White

1=Green          2=Blue          3=Yellow          4= Pink
5=Orange         6=Purple        7=White

1=Yellow    2=Brown    3=Pink    4= Blue

5=Orange    6=Purple    7=Red

1=Green   2=White   3=Yellow   4= Blue

5=Orange   6=Purple   7=Pink   8=Red

1=Green          2=Red          3=Yellow          4= Blue

5=Orange          6=Purple          7=Pink          8=Brown

1=Blue         2=Pink         3=Yellow       4= Purple
5=Orange       6=White        7=Green

| 1=Red | 2=Brown | 3=Yellow | 4= Blue |
| 5=Orange | 6=Purple | 7=Pink | 8=White |

1=Green 2=Red 3=Yellow 4= Blue
5=Orange 6=Purple 7=Pink 8=White

1=Green        2=Brown        3=Yellow        4= Blue

5=Orange       6=Purple       7=Pink         8=Red

1=Green        2=Brown        3=Yellow        4= Blue

5=Orange        6=Purple        7=Pink

1=Green          2=Brown          3=Yellow          4= Blue

5=Orange          6=Purple          7=Pink          8=Red

1=Green        2=Brown        3=Yellow        4= Blue

5=Orange       6=Purple        7=Pink

1=Green        2=Brown        3=Yellow        4= Blue
5=Orange        6=Purple        7=Pink        8=White

1=Green    2=Purple    3=Yellow    4= Blue

5=Orange    6=Pink    7=Red

1=Yellow 2=Pink 3=Purple 4= Green
5=Orange 6=Blue 7=White 8=Red

1=Green 2=Brown 3=Yellow 4= Blue

5=Orange 6=Purple 7=Pink 8=White

1=Pink        2=Yellow        3=Orange        4= Blue

5=Purple        6=White        7=Red